SELF-DISCOVERY JOURNAL FOR WOMEN

250 Journal Questions and Writing Prompts
to Find Yourself and to Awaken Your
Divine Feminine

by Evelyn K. Lim

Text Copyright © EvelynLim.com

All rights reserved. No part of this guide may be reproduced in any form without permission in writing from the publisher except in the case of brief quotations embodied in critical articles or reviews.

Legal & Disclaimer

The information contained in this book and its contents is not designed to replace or take the place of any form of medical or professional advice; and is not meant to replace the need for independent medical, financial, legal or other professional advice or services, as may be required. The content and information in this book has been provided for educational and entertainment purposes only.

The content and information contained in this book has been compiled from sources deemed reliable, and it is accurate to the best of the Author's knowledge, information, and belief. However, the Author cannot guarantee its accuracy and validity and cannot be held liable for any errors and/or omissions. Further changes are periodically made to this book as and when needed. Where appropriate and/or necessary, you must consult a professional (including but not limited to your doctor, attorney, financial advisor or such other professional advisor) before using any of the suggested remedies, techniques, or information in this book.

Upon using the contents and information contained in this book, you agree to hold harmless the Author from and against any damages, costs, and expenses, including any legal fees potentially resulting from the application of any of the information provided by this book. This disclaimer applies to any loss, damages or injury caused by the use and application, whether directly or indirectly, of any advice or information presented, whether for breach of contract, tort, negligence, personal injury, criminal intent, or under any other cause of action.

You agree to accept all risks of using the information presented inside this book.

You agree that by continuing to read this book, where appropriate and/or necessary, you shall consult a professional (including but not limited to your doctor, attorney, or financial advisor or such other advisor as needed) before using any of the suggested remedies, techniques, or information in this book.

Dedication

I dedicate this book to my mother.

Even though words often fail me, I'd like you to know that I love you very much.

Thank you for your delicious cooking, and your love and care all these years.

Table of Contents

Introduction – Your Search for Answers 7
    You Can Begin in Your Own Home 9
    Why Is The Self-Discovery Journey Important for Women 10

Chapter 1 – What is Journaling and Why Journal 16
    What is Journaling? 17
    Journaling for Self-Discovery 18
    The Research That Backs Journaling 22
    Commit to Carving out the Time 24

Chapter 2 – Self-Discovery for Women or the Divine Feminine 26
    Your Divine Feminine or Nature 26
    Awakening Your Divine Feminine 30

Chapter 3 Journaling Essentials 34
    How to Journal 34
    Setting Up a Sacred Space for Journaling 36
    Guidelines for Journaling 38

Chapter 3 – 50 Journal Prompts To Start for Self-Discovery 46
    50 Journal Questions to Start 47

Chapter 4 – 50 Journal Prompts for Your Inner Therapist 64
    50 Journal Questions for Restoring Inner Balance 65

Chapter 5 – 60 Journal Prompts for Connecting with Your Sacred Feminine Power 83
    53 Journal Questions for Embracing Your Divine Feminine 88
    7 Questions For Connecting with Your Chakras 106

Chapter 5 – 50 Journal Prompts for Knowing Yourself Via Relationships 113
50 Journal Questions on Relationships *115*

Chapter 6 – 20 Journal Questions for Knowing Yourself Via Work Life 132
20 Journal Questions about Work Life *133*

Chapter 7 – 20 Journal Questions for Aligning with Purpose & Spiritual Consciousness 140
20 Journal Questions on Purpose & Spiritual Consciousness *141*

Chapter 8 – Journaling Review 148
Review Your Objectives *148*
Review What You Have Written *149*
Reviewing Your Journaling Experience *150*

Chapter 9 - Lessons for the Divine Feminine 152
Creative Power *152*
Cosmic Womb *153*
The Integration of Masculine and Feminine Energies *154*

Conclusion – Journaling for Sacred Self-Discovery 156
Benefits of Journaling *156*
Journaling: The Way for Spiritual Transformation *159*
Awaken, Activate and Access Your Sacred Feminine Power *160*
From Sacred Self-Discovery to Tapping into Source *162*

Claim Your Free Gifts 164

Check Out Other Books 165

About The Author 166

Introduction – Your Search for Answers

Would you like to discover more about who you are?

Have you been struck by a bolt that awakens you to the fact that you don't really know much about yourself at a deeper level?

Now that you are ready to shine more light into self-discovery, you also realize that you are facing darkness.

You've not been able to put a finger on what's missing; yet, you are increasingly aware that there's a gaping hole from deep inside.

What is it? You can't quite figure out what's best to do next. Take another personality test? Consult an astrologer? Look up the family tree? Then again, nothing you've done so far had fully quelled the ache of "not knowing".

What you do know, however, is that you've been tuning into an underlying sense of unhappiness and you've been carrying a melancholic feeling for the longest time.

And so, you would like to have better answers for a change.

Your search for clarity might have been triggered by external events too.

It might have been a marriage collapse, a relationship breakdown or a business failure that led you on your self-discovery path.

Or it could be that you simply got sick and tired of the pain of not having a strong sense of self or esteem.

In the throes of your pain, you have decided that enough is enough!

You've got enough of feeling horribly unsettled, anxious and confused from a lack in direction.

Whatever the situation was, you have been called to question the fabric of your existence.

The questions you wrestle with: *Who am I? What do I truly want? What's my purpose in life?*

Well, I'd like to help by pointing you a way to get answers.

I have got *GREAT* news.

The great news is that you do not need to take off on an expensive "Eat Pray Love" round-the world trip, attend a meditation retreat in the deep forest or join a Wild Women Sisterhood circle to reclaim yourself immediately.

There is no need for you to book a plane ticket. Or, a need for you to set aside money for travel. No more looking elsewhere either.

Your epic quintessential self-discovery journey can happen right in your own home. *With a pen and some journaling paper.* As spiritual masters tell you, the search takes place from within.

You Can Begin in Your Own Home

Who is she that you are hoping to discover? She is right inside you. Respond to her call to find her. She has the answers to the questions that you seek. In fact, she's been waiting for you; scared, alone and afraid to speak.

"The union of feminine and masculine energies within the individual is the basis of all creation."— Shakti Gawain

Fortunately, you exist at a time where you can give yourself permission to reclaim yourself without being judged, criticized or shamed. Times have changed since the days when women or feminine energy is considered inferior. More and more women are becoming aware that they can show up, be visible and express with an open heart.

Notwithstanding, be aware that celebrating your female or womanly strength is not a New Age trend. Nor is it just some esoteric practice, where you sit in a sacred circle while chanting mantras. In fact, I believe that it makes common sense to embrace who you are. When you do, your confidence increases and potentially, your ability to align with your highest potential and lead a fuller life too.

In the meantime, may I be permitted to suggest: A big part of your "not knowing" ache comes from having missed, abandoned or shelving the Divine Feminine aside.

Hence, your first task is to find her.

She may not be easy to find, in the beginning.

After all, she represents shadow pieces about you that have been left behind. It may be that you've forgotten about her desires and needs, or even her existence. Self-discovery helps you to uncover what's been hidden, suppressed and unacknowledged.

You have to nudge her out. Let her know that she's safe. Tell her that you are ok with her broken English, poor writing and bad spelling mistakes. You are to embrace her wholeheartedly. All of which can be accomplished through a simple process known as *Journaling*!

"I wasn't searching for something or someone….I was searching for me." Carrie Bradshaw

Why Is The Self-Discovery Journey Important for Women

Before I proceed with the rest of my book, I would like to put you at ease.

May I ask: do you feel uncomfortable when I use the phrase "Divine Feminine"?

Well, there is nothing to be afraid of. Don't misunderstand. I am not about to ask you to channel Goddess Lakshmi or dance tantric for exploring your sexuality. While the phrase "Divine Feminine" tends to be associated with new age, the need to connect with and embrace your feminine side should not be lost.

In this book, I will be using the phrases "Divine Feminine" and "Feminine Divine". With these phrases, I simply mean to delve into your feminine nature. As you happen to be a spiritual being, I have also used the word "divine". You see, the "Divine Feminine" phrase first came to me inspiredly when I was writing the first few pages of this book during the wee hours of the morning. Soon, other inspired ideas that help me develop this journaling guide flowed.

There will be times when I use the words "Feminine Nature", "Feminine Energy" and "Feminine Power" interchangeably too. Hence, if you prefer and find them more acceptable, you can replace the word "Divine" with "Nature", "Energy" or "Power" in my writings. In short, do what makes you feel comfortable.

As I've indicated, it's far more important to develop the understanding on why it serves you to find yourself and to discover your feminine nature. A review into the factors that prevent women from knowing their true selves is going to help. Now that we have put the matter on phrases and labels used aside, allow me to explain further.

Throughout history, men had subjugated women. Women were dependent on men for food and shelter and they were treated like objects. Many women were also robbed of their basic human rights. Collectively, the energetic distortions and illusions of mistaken beliefs hang like an overcast cloud, even though much has changed in terms of female empowerment over the last millennia.

These distorted patterns had left women traumatized, invisible, shamed and abused. The patterns seep into societal consciousness. While you may not have personally experienced huge traumas in your life, it's highly possible for your psyche to be affected too. Simply because you are part of society! You can easily understand how pervasive the patterns are, by going online where there is a widespread of suggestive pornographic pictures with women portrayed as submissive and ready to please.

Should you think back, you may realize that you've been conditioned since you were young to behave or to buy into certain beliefs because of your gender. For example, you could have been told, "Girls cannot climb trees and be tomboys!" I've heard my fair share of being told what to do and what not to do because I was born a girl.

Don't be mistaken. I am not blaming my parents and grandmother who had a lot of traditional ideas about how a female should behave. They inherited a whole bunch of limiting messages and beliefs from their parents. And it's probably the same for you with your parents and grandparents too.

What if you can remove the shackles that have prevented you from self-actualization? It's very possible that in your desire to be accepted by family, friends and even your spouse, you've buried the true you underneath. You will need to reclaim who you innately are. And it comes at no better time than now!

"There is a collective force rising up on the earth today, an energy of the reborn feminine ... This is a time of monumental shift, from the male dominance of human consciousness back to a balanced relationship between masculine and feminine." — Marianne Williamson

There was once I had lived with the discomforting drum of "not knowing". The discomfort had settled shortly after I allowed the madness of trying to find myself in external pursuits die. Soon, it became a painful ache, when I realized how unfulfilling it was to go to drinking parties in a bid to fit in with the crowd. I discovered that I hardly knew who I was.

To resolve the ache, I found out that I had to first learn to love and accept myself unconditionally (check out my book Self-Love Secrets that I eventually wrote). Emotional healing freed me. And with the freedom, I realized that I was free to express myself in whatever way I wanted. I could write, for instance.

Journaling quickly became an amazing tool that offered me not just an outlet for release, but as a way of accessing deeper personal truths. Today, my ideas on creation and spirituality are drawn from contemplative reflections, having given birth to two lovely girls, learning from spiritual masters, walking from darkness to dawn and a sprinkle of soul awareness. So here is what I'd like to lay out…

You are a female embodiment of the divine. In case your memory has been blocked by amnesia, your soul agreement is to authentically express the sacred feminine in this physical incarnation. Your individual purpose is to embrace all the disparate parts of the Divine Feminine, so that you can be in oneness.

Oneness means integrating both your divine feminine and masculine energies. There is no separation. Both sides are complementary to each other. As such, any distorted patterns created by a masculine world needs to be repaired.

Just imagine having the ability to create a life based on your true self, drawing on your sacred gifts and knowing what you truly want? I bet you'd feel a lot happier, purposeful and fulfilled. If I may say so, by picking up this book, you are giving yourself the opportunity to discover your true nature. By committing to the journaling process as outlined, you will be rewarded.

Journaling gives you a voice where you have found it hard to express yourself before. Answering each journal prompt is like having an intimate conversation with your soul. You are free to strip away the layers of masks as you dive in through a process of self-inquiry. Who are you outside the carefully curated life that you display on social media such as Facebook and Instagram?

Journaling is Chocolate melting away the sense of discomfort from keeping it all in. No more pretenses, trying to keep up with the Joneses or fitting in with the Janes. Any initial discomfort from processing negative emotions or limiting thoughts that you write about will gradually dissolve to a sense of freedom.

I believe what's left there - after the stripping, peeling and melting - will soothe your soul. It was exactly what happened to me. The more you dive into the writing process, the more warmly satiated you are going to feel.

The process of self-inquiry takes courage. You are to bare your soul, expose yourself and own up to your shortcomings before you can arrive at some meaningful answers. Insight usually arises at the point where heart, mind, and spirit meet in your soul awakening.

"Knowing yourself is the beginning of all wisdom."
Aristotle

Interested to experience for yourself? Great! I applaud you for being brave.

Let's get even more comfortable. Go grab a cup of warm Chamomile tea. Kick off your Prada heels. Put on some relaxing music. Diffuse lavender essential oil in the air and inhale deeply.

In the *Spirit of Sisterhood*, allow me to take you by the hand on a journaling journey! I invite you to begin this exciting adventure by setting an intention. Here's what you can say...

"As I journal, I give myself the permission to feel safe, to explore, to accept, to love and to know myself deeply."

Chapter 1 – What is Journaling and Why Journal

Personality and strength finder tests are helpful for self-discovery. Getting a Nadi leaf reading too. They offer pieces of information that solves part of the puzzle to the mystery of "who am I". However, these methods do not reveal aspects that journaling can cover. Nor do they also culminate in a soul-satisfying experience that connects you with your Divine Feminine from the inside.

Meditation is often recommended as a way to discover the Ultimate Truth. It is very much an experiential process whereby you'd need to sit quietly and tune in for answers yourself. Even though there are books, masters or teachers who share their findings, the answers that you seek are far more likely to hit home when you find them yourself.

As you may have realized by now, meditation is not something that is easy to start. It's not, when your mind is busy like a superhighway. Mostly, your mind is anywhere but in the present. Also, meditating may not let you know what your strengths, talents, and passions are. Yet, awareness of these aspects can help you better navigate life in the meantime.

Hence, an easier route for self-discovery is to start with journaling. Through journaling, you can get to know more about yourself, your gifts and authentic dreams. Like meditation, journaling is experiential. What's wonderful is that you can apply mindfulness with journaling, for self-discovery.

With mindfulness journaling, you engage your thoughts, emotions and body responses. You notice your feelings, you become aware of what you think and the conclusions that you have made about the world. By recounting your responses to life through journaling, you give your opportunity to pause and reflect. You are encouraged to slow down and to contemplate over the topic at hand.

Journaling is seeing renewed popularity. You can attribute it to the internet's ease of getting a journal published, that is via blogging. However, journaling whether through written words or pictures has been happening for eons. Think about cave drawings! Your urge to record and explore through personal writings is nothing unusual, therefore, it is time-honored and universal.

What is Journaling?

What is journaling, exactly? Some might picture a diary, a small volume bound with a lock and often full of secret romance. To others, the idea of a journal is like a ship's log, recording progress through a particular journey. These are both examples of journaling, though their purposes are very different.

Maybe the only definition you can confidently suggest for journaling is that it is a regular practice of written reflections or commentary. The operative word here is "regular." Your writing does not form a journal unless it involves successive entries over a period of time.

If nothing else, journaling requires you to form a habit. It's a discipline that requires some dedication. It can certainly be a one-time effort, but you won't be able to reap enough benefits especially if you are hoping to journal for self-discovery.

Journal writing can be about anything you feel inclined to write. At its most basic, you can journal any experience, from your Army Boot Camp to your teenage romance with your first boyfriend, from your search for work to your vacation in the mountains, from getting married to your first day as a mother. You can just write randomly to express yourself.

Or you can take your journaling experience one step further by intending it for self-discovery. Your reasons for journaling may include specific objectives such as:

- make a change
- improve my attitude
- increase my emotional intelligence
- find something to believe in
- figure out why I keep making the same mistakes over and over.

Hence, you may want to start off by reflecting over what your specific objective is. The writing prompts, presented as questions in this book, are designed to trigger your thoughts for overall self-discovery. It is an excellent companion for your journey in getting to know yourself better. Outside of the voices of your parents, spouse, partner, friends and so on, you are to find your own.

Journaling for Self-Discovery

As mentioned, that ache of emptiness, "not knowing" or discomforting pit in your stomach that you have, can be addressed through journaling. It's certainly what I had discovered when I started to put thoughts on paper. I revel in the writing process for self-discovery. Writing became an outlet, much akin to how drawing is like for visual artists.

Journaling has been called a "near-perfect hobby." I like to think of it as my psycho-spiritual practice. It helped me deal with some of my darkest thoughts. And I mean, like really dark. There were times when I felt low. Writing was one exercise that consistently helped me with making sense of what I was thinking.

A daily journaling practice can provide a way to greater self-knowledge, self-acceptance, and compassion for others. Your journal serves as a friend, a confidant, and even a readily-available therapist. You can use your journal to process what happened today or what occurred decades ago that may still be impacting your life.

In your journal, you can reflect, clarify, explore or even rage. It's your haven of safety. No one needs to know your secret thoughts. Answering the right self-discovery questions can be a powerful way to get to know who you are at core, challenge false beliefs about your identity and get clear about what you truly want for your life.

Most of us have been strongly conditioned by early childhood experiences. So much so that we act out of unconscious patterns of our troubled past. Were we betrayed, lied to, shamed, made fun of or judged by people we looked up to when we were young? We fail to stop and question if they are still impacting us today. We lose sight of ourselves in the process.

Have you ever taken the time to listen to what your true nature is really like?

It's okay if you haven't. Few of us has never made time for intentional self-discovery. It was the case for me until I became conscious of the fact that I knew so little about myself. Previously, I had been bombarded with opinions from other people—what they think of me, how they perceive me, what they want for me —that I forgot to include the one voice that matters. My own! Sounds familiar?

It can be difficult to understand who you are without processing your life journey. For self-disovery, you have to become aware of your developments, of the influences that affect you, the experiences that formed you, of who you were in the past, who you are now and who you want to be in the future. And you can do so through journaling.

Through contemplation, you are able to identify what you have been stubbornly attached to and what no longer serves you. By becoming aware, you are more willing to let go of your illusions and negative perceptions. You may also realize that the stories that you created in your head are temporary. What caused you to be so angry about one day is replaced by another set of events that bring you joy on another day. Your emotions can change. And so do your thoughts.

As you develop deeper awareness, you are being asked to answer to the call of shedding your emotional attachments and limiting beliefs have sabotaged your happiness and well-being. You will realize that it is in your best interest to release all that no longer serves you.

Releasing does not mean that you give up your Chanel bag or that you throw away your Ferragamo shoes right away. Neither does it mean giving up your dreams for a better life. Conversely, releasing simply means that you are aware that you no longer need them to bring you happiness right now. You certainly don't need them to show off or boost your ego in front of others.

Then again, it does not mean that you no longer allow yourself the pleasure of experiences. May I contend that there is nothing wrong if you decide to treat yourself to gourmet meals. Or, if you buy something luxurious to wear as long as you can well afford it.

More importantly, releasing is about giving up your obsession with materialistic desires and things that do not truly matter. You give up your obsession because you know that the constant craving is making you sick. Thus, the choice that you make is to be happy - no matter what!

Once you have made the decision, craving for the next it-bag or diamond ring simply disappears in a column of smoke. You are more than just a designer label or someone with a shopping obsession. You may also realize that you are more than any role defined by society. Nor do you need to fit into societal's expectations or standards.

Through the journal prompts laid out in the following chapters, you will be invited to explore letting go. You can learn from your life lessons, how you have lost yourself in your made-up stories and the changes that you can make for greater peace, harmony, and happiness. Amazingly, in the process of letting go who you are not, you can potentially be led to the consciousness of who you may truly be.

Journaling is very much a spiritual process. It is one that allows you to express your authentic self. And one that supports your evolution.

The Research That Backs Journaling

Is journaling still sounding hokey to you? Perhaps you are not used to some of the seemingly "spiritual woo woo" terms that I have been using. Or it may be that you simply want to know something more substantiated to justify why you need to make journaling a new habit.

Well, allow me to share with you some research findings that back up journaling.

For a start, studies show that our short-term memory storage is limited. We can hold only five or six, maybe seven items in our head at a time. Hence, any number beyond that, we start to sweat and feel overwhelmed.

When you clear out the storage from your mental brain, it becomes quieter. Your mind stops functioning like a broken recorder, playing the same material over and over again. Reviewing your journal thoughts on paper becomes a lot easier. You are able to identify the repetitive thoughts that have been preventing you from moving forward.

Psychologists say that journaling offers you a chance to reframe your personal narrative. If you check in with heightened awareness, you would have realized that your personal narrative is often filtered by your beliefs and emotions. Hence, the story in your mind may not be totally true. *Journaling offers you the chance to clarify, edit, and find new meaning in your narrative.* As I have found, it's possible to transform a story of pain into power!

A study conducted at Stanford University involved African-American students who were struggling to adjust to college life. The students were divided into two groups. One group was asked to produce an essay or video about what college was like. Their creations were to be shown to future students. The findings were that those who reflected on their experiences through writing or video received significantly better grades in the following months than their peers in the control group.

Dr. James W. Pennebaker, a social psychologist at the University of Texas at Austin who is considered the pioneer of writing therapy, shared there isn't one answer on why journaling works. In a landmark 1988 study and as outlined in his book "Opening Up: The Healing Power of Expressing Emotion", students were assigned the homework of writing about either traumatic experiences or superficial topics. They had to do this for four days in a row.

Six weeks after the writing sessions, it was found that those who had written about their traumatic experiences reported more positive mood and fewer illnesses as compared to those who had simply written about everyday experiences.

More recently, in a 2013 Psychosomatic Medicine publication, Elizabeth Broadbent, professor of medicine at the University of Auckland in New Zealand and co-author of the study, reported that research was conducted on whether expressive writing could help older adults heal faster after a medically necessary biopsy. In the study, 49 healthy adults wrote about either upsetting events or daily activities for 20 minutes, three days in a row.

A time lag of two weeks was introduced to ensure any initial negative feelings stirred up by recalling upsetting events had passed. Then, the participants had a biopsy on the arm, and photographs over the next 21 days tracked the healing. On the 11th day, 76 percent of the group that did expressive writing had fully healed as compared with 42 percent of the control group. It was postulated that the writing in Broadbent's study may have also sped recovery by improving sleep, thus speeding up wound healing.

In the same year, a paper in the British Journal of Health Psychology, also found that writing about an emotional topic lowered participants' cortisol levels.

There are plenty more research studies conducted that backup journaling. So, here you go! Lots of juicy reasons why journaling may be what you need!

Commit to Carving out the Time

Journaling takes time, but it can also make time. Regular journalers go through their days focused with fewer distracting thoughts, and they have more energy. You'll have to journal over the next few weeks to see the difference. Trust the process! It works!

Make a commitment to yourself that you will write at least 10 minutes everyday, for a start. I suggest journaling in the early morning. Julia Cameron, author of The Artist's Way, calls the journaling practice she recommends the "morning pages." I personally find journaling a great way to start the day before the frenzy of activities begins.

If mornings do not work for you, set aside another time. Late evening before you sleep could be another good slot. Setting aside the same time each day to write will make it easier to remember. You'd be a lot motivated when you make journaling a ritual.

It is important to keep to journaling. Journaling helps you to slow down. It's a chance for you to take stock before life passes you by. *Let journaling be the avenue for you to reflect on your experiences, regain balance and to take charge of your life!*

"Writing is a spiritual practice in that people that have no spiritual path can undertake it and, as they write, they begin to wake up to a larger connection. After a while, people tend to find that there is some muse that they are connecting to." Julia Cameron, The Artist's Way.

Chapter 2 – Self-Discovery for Women or the Divine Feminine

Your Divine Feminine or Nature

Now that we know more about the general benefits of journaling, let's understand even more about why journaling is perfect for women and for connecting with your Feminine Nature!

Be aware that the Divine Feminine is not bound to gender. It lives in all of us – males and females alike. We are to embrace the sacredness of our feminine nature, whether we are a male or female.

However, because of the consciousness that comes along with the female body, women are more pre-disposed to drawing on her feminine attributes. Look, let's accept the fact that we are born with two X chromosomes and that we have a womb. We are built to develop breasts at a certain age. The female body is the vessel that helps us express our feminine nature to its fullest.

I've written this journal guide generally for women . However, it's possible that you are male or/and somone who wishes to explore your feminine nature, using this book. That's fine too. Simply use the sections or parts that serve you.

Positive feminine energy is about intuition, nurture, receptivity, and creativity. On the other hand, positive masculine energy is associated with leadership, logic, assertiveness and conviction. For whole-life living, drawing on the two sets of energy will help you align with your highest potential.

The Lost Art of Connecting with Your Feminine Energy

Unfortunately, the practice of connecting with our innate feminine qualities is a lost art until recent times. Why it is a lost art is because of the predominantly masculine world that we live in. You are likely to find that you have been relying more on your masculine energy to navigate life.

Masculine energy is needed in the boardroom and for getting things done. You need masculine energy to negotiate with those that have more masculine energy. And as my professional female friends tell me, they are encouraged to show up with masculine power in the workplace anyway.

However, for optimal living and success, you wouldn't want to miss out on accessing your feminine power too. Don't be mistaken. Feminine power is not about applying make-up, enhancing the size of your boobs or dressing seductively. It is certainly not about using your feminine wiles to manipulate the males for gaining ahead either.

In appropriate situations, drawing on your feminine energy could be more helpful than relying on masculine energy alone. For instance, you may want to use intuition to guide you when designing a proposal to pitch to your customers but when it comes to establishing strategies, you may want to draw on your masculine energy for precision in planning. In other words, you will be served by integrating both these energies within you.

Unfortunately, you may have found it difficult to do so. It could be that you have been plugged into negative energies affecting women in the collective consciousness that cloud over time. As mentioned, women had been bullied, shamed and oppressed by men through history. They had been objectified, with their worth severely reduced according to their physical appearance. Women had been stripped of their self-esteem, confidence, and respect. Eating disorders affect more women than men, for one.

Look, I am not about to bash men. What I am more interested in is how we can help ourselves to heal and reclaim our sovereignty. If every one of us can take personal responsibility, we contribute to the collective consciousness that evolves. Our children will see better days, with none of the illusions and distortions that have been inherited over past generations.

Many women had been caught in the virtue trap. Sadly, a number continue to hold the thinking that they need to have perfect virtues, perfect bodies and lead perfect lives. They adopt standards of perfection that are not achievable. And when they don't achieve these high standards, they whip themselves. They drive themselves nuts attempting to please or to conform to other people's standards: how they should behave, dress, look and feel.

"Nobody objects to a woman being a good writer or sculptor or geneticists if at the same time she manages to be a good wife, a good mother, a good-looking, good-tempered, well-groomed and unaggressive." Leslie M Mcintyre

What is probably the case is that you may not have realized how destructive the negative patterns can be and how they could have affected you until now. I certainly did not have a clue until I started to work on myself. It was also when I found out that I carried false assumptions about how men and women should behave and be like.

Where some of these assumptions came from, I did not know. They certainly did not come directly from my parents or caregivers. Then, to my surprise, when I began to investigate, I discovered that I had unknowingly adopted layers and layers of conditioning from having tapped into societal consciousness.

No wonder why I was having a hard time trying to will myself out of "I am not good enough". I was unconsciously carrying some very distorted ideas on why women should be inferior to men. Later, when I started working with clients, I found out that many of the women had similar issues as well.

As children, many of us have been conditioned to hate our emotions, to repress them, to deny them and so on. We could also be given the message that crying is a sign of weakness and that only females are allowed to cry. Thus, we grow up with the idea that negative emotions are bad, that they are wrong and that we should not experience them. The conditioning is deeply embedded in our psyche.

If you are connected to your Feminine Energy, you may find yourself more connected with your emotions as compared to the males. Hence, by being more prone to crying or showing your sadness, you may have perceived yourself to be the weaker sex. Can you imagine closing and telling yourself not to feel because you don't want to be seen as weak or emotional?

Feminine Energy is also linked to water. Water is related to flow. It is an element of the emotional world. Yet, at the same time, feminine energy is full of grace. It is about creativity and intuition as well. Thus, when you block yourself from feelings, your feminine gifts no longer become accessible to you. If you don't trust or believe that you are creative and intuitive, you will not be able to draw on these gifts.

Often enough, these gifts - especially intuition - are not encouraged in a predominantly masculine world that emphasizes logic and reasoning. In fact, you may have shut them down for fear of ridicule. Yet, by being blocked, you can find it difficult to write, paint, dance or even problem solve – even where both creativity and intuition could otherwise help you come up with a better solution.

It's imperative that you correct any false and mistaken ideas. To be able to feel is natural. It is what makes you human. When you don't give yourself the opportunity to feel, you suffer. Stuffing your emotions can lead to depression. You may also fall ill. Your well-being gets lowered. No one, not even the men, stands to benefit when this happens.

Awakening Your Divine Feminine

Journaling is a way that can help you reclaim yourself, where there are parts that have been abandoned, suppressed or forgotten. You are invited to acknowledge what you feel. Angry, lazy, indifferent, doubtful, confused, insecure, painful and so on. Even if you do not like feeling negative emotions, you are to acknowledge that you have them.

Acknowledging does not mean that you justify your reactions. It simply means that you are aware that you have negative emotions. You embrace yourself anyway while holding the space to let them go.

You also give yourself the opportunity to examine your beliefs. Beliefs are formed from undergoing events in your life. Some help to empower you and some hold you back from being the best that you can be.

As mentioned, there are also the illusions that you had adopted by being part of the collective conscious. Beliefs that no longer serve you are like "women are the weaker sex", "girls cannot be doctors but nurses" and "wait for Prince Charming to come rescue you". By knowing what your limiting ones are, you are able to correct them.

Awakening your Divine Feminine helps you to ultimately reclaim who you innately are. Please know that you don't have to be "good" or "virtuous" before you can meet her from within. In fact, you are encouraged to throw away all the labels and forms that do not serve you. You are already perfection at source.

At the highest level, when you access your Feminine Nature, you are getting in touch with your soul who plays a part in creation. It's not a small matter if you ask me. You have the co-creative power to birth a divine spark into being, from the non-physical into reality. That's incredible, don't you think?

"I learned that the real creator was my inner Self, the Shakti….that desire to do something is God inside talking through us." Michelle Shea

When you activate the Sacred Feminine, you are also awakening shakti, the fundamental creative power of the universe. It is through her that you recognize the sacredness of embodiment here on Earth. While the shakti manifests through meditation and yoga, journaling helps you to become awake to your feminine true nature.

Your highest power is the power to connect Source and the manifested world. You are the midwife of creation. Hence, you play an important role. Without you, there will be no continuity in the human race. With this awareness, you are to acknowledge the importance in the part that you play. How can you allow anyone to tell you anything less?

The Divine Feminine's ability to birth babies sounds awesome but how does it apply to you if you are not drawn to having a baby in this life? So does this mean that this becomes less of a superpower as it can't be utilized in such cases?

On the contrary, no. Manifestation is not limited to activating your co-creative power to give birth to a child. If anything, manifesting is essentially about birthing what is from the non-physical to the physical world. You may want to channel your creative ability for launching your inspired idea, project or business. Hence, if you are blocked from connecting with your feminine energy, healing or repair needs to happen. Otherwise, you are going to face challenges.

How journaling can help is for you to bring awareness to your feminine gifts. Through reflection using some of the writing prompts in this book, you can examine your various roles in society – as a mother, partner in a relationship, friend or for work and career. The writing prompts can help you with identifying some of the distortions in beliefs and illusions, especially if you answer the questions truthfully. It's how you can get insights for aligning with your highest potential.

Self-discovery gets you tapped into your essential nature. You learn not only to embrace your Divine Feminine where she has stayed hidden but with love, to channel her into the light. You draw on her strengths and awaken her purpose, where it was dead before. Now that she is centered, aware, very much alive and strong, she is truly in her power. You are her. And she is you.

Just imagine, by integrating both your masculine and feminine parts for navigating the world, you enhance your capacity to lead a full life.

Chapter 3 Journaling Essentials

How to Journal

You can journal by hand, type, set up a blog or draw. Find out how you can journal and pick the way that fits your preference.

Journaling by Hand

1. Assemble your tools. I prefer an 8 ½" x 11" spiral notebook that will open flat rather than one of the smaller, hardback blank books. Whatever you choose, find a journal that's attractive to you, but don't buy a journal so fancy that you feel your writing must match its perfection. Journaling can be a messy exercise, with lots of scratch outs, misspelled words and wrong punctuation. It's completely okay!

2. Find a pen that feels just right to you. If you don't have a favorite pen, enjoy shopping for just the right refillable one, and don't use it for any other purpose.

3. You may also want to have colored pens or highlighter on hand. These can be used for emphasizing certain words or you may also use them for making your journal more colorful.

Journaling by Typing

While most journal books advocate that you journal by hand, I beg to differ. I had found both writing and typing out my thoughts at various times, just as rewarding. So, my suggestion is to choose the medium that is most conducive.

I prefer to type out my thoughts on my personal laptop. However, you may wish to create an online journal through blogging. Go over to blogger.com for a free account. Just remember to set it to private, if you don't want anyone else to read your writing.

Journaling with Drawings

Journaling your answers need not solely be in written form. Add loops, lines, circles, arrows or any drawings if you want to. You are allowed to cultivate a sense of play and you don't need to have neat rows of words every time.

What's important is allowing yourself the opportunity to convey what's inside you, through journaling. If an image, symbol or sign flash in your mind, it may just be a lot easier for you to draw it out instead of describing it in words. In short, discover the artist from within.

It's certainly what my girl does. She fills her journals with comic drawings that depict her inner world. Her way of journaling gives her a chance to process her thoughts and emotions. It's how she restores her balance amidst a demanding school life. I encourage you to let your inner artist play.

Setting Up a Sacred Space for Journaling

Journaling is as sacred as you decide to make it be. Here are some recommendations for you...

1. Find a comfortable place. If possible, write in the same place everyday. It becomes your dedicated place for journaling.

2. Put your handphone on silent mode, to avoid distractions and having to take incoming unimportant calls.

3. Play some soft music if it helps you get into the flow. Or, if you prefer, let silence be your friend.

4. Sniff the same essential oil, such as lavender, before journaling can help relax you. Getting your diffuser going acts as a subconscious reminder that it's time to write.

5. Have a cup of your favorite drink on the desk. Tea, coffee, lemon water, whatever – get this ready.

6. Hold on to your crystals or have them nearby if you prefer. The idea is to set up a sacred space for journaling.

7. Invoke an intention. You can say it in the form of a prayer to God, the Universe or Divine Source. Saying a prayer is nothing religious. Rather, you are acknowledging that there is an overarching universal life force and that you are spirit. Remember God or Source is both within and outside of you.

For the prayer of intention, you can use your own words or the one below...

Dear God, the Universe or Divine Source, I dedicate this sacred journaling space to you. I feel safe and I am ready to express myself. Let love take over my writing. I surrender and allow you to be the source of what I need to know. Open me to what I am meant to receive from this journaling exercise. Release me from what I need to let go of. Guide me with your messages. Show me what I need to learn. I commit my full presence and I am one with you. Thank you!

The more pleasant you make your journaling ritual, the more you will look forward to it and the easier it will be to establish your practice.

Guidelines for Journaling

1. Make "Me" Time a Priority

Dedicating to a journal writing practice means allocating time on a very regular basis, away from others and bringing attention to the self. You may worry that you're being selfish. Some of the people around you may disapprove or want your attention.

Well, if you don't make journaling an important priority, the exercise rapidly drops to the bottom of your to-do list. You won't ever journal unless you actually sit down with your notebook and pen. That may seem simple enough but in reality, unless you deem it important, you won't allocate time for it.

The common sense of journaling is very close to the common sense of meditating. Our frenzied forward motion needs commensurate quiet time. It helps you to restore balance. To journal, you must have enough self-awareness to sidestep your various excuses, remove distractions and to get to the page.

Your Divine Feminine seeks expression. She can only do so when you create allocate time for her. Hence, give her what she needs. *Journaling ultimately leads you to soul integration.* In short, it creates a healthier You!

Neglecting the practice is actually inconsiderate of both yourself and those around you. It's important "me" time. Let others know that you are undertaking self-care. They will learn to get out of your way, once they start to realise how much happier and calmer you've become.

2. Do Not Judge Yourself or Your Writing!

Unlike any other writing you may have done, this type journaling is all about the process and NOT about the product.

You journal for the act of journaling—to get your thoughts and feelings down on paper. Hence, it does not matter in what format, if the grammar is correct, if it's neat, or if all the words are spelled right. Your sentence structure does not need to be perfect.

By focusing on the process of journaling rather than what you are writing, you can freely express whatever emotions you are feeling. You will often find that as you write about uncomfortable feelings, they dissipate. By writing, you have the opportunity to express your true feelings. As you sit with them, you will realize that they are fleeting.

Hence, avoid self-judgment. Instead, hold an inviting space. Get in touch with the part that has been suppressed for a long time and allow her to speak without interruption. At this point, you may want to keep your journal private. Don't share it with anyone who's likely to judge or criticize you or your writing.

3. Feeling Safe to Express Freely

The best way to begin a journal practice is just to start writing! Stop over-analyzing for a start. Write what is on your mind—your hopes, fears, doubts, dreams, job, relationships, children, old hurts, what's going on in the world—anything that you need to express is a good topic for today's entry in your journal. In other words, begin with a mental dump!

While you may choose to write about what you did on any given day, journaling for self-discovery is more about what you are feeling than what you are doing. You will find that if you keep your writing in first person, it will be easier to get in touch with how you are really feeling about an issue.

Be aware when you are drifting away from first person. It's possible for this to happen especially if you tend to avoid your feelings. For example, if you write

"We often think that…" try to switch to "I often think…" or even better "I often feel…"

In this way, you are compelled to own your own feelings. Commit to getting more authentic and real in your writing. It's critical that you are honest with yourself. Even if you think your answers may make you look bad or evil, they don't take away your true essence. Trust me!

As you write, peel back the layers of your thoughts and begin to see your feelings more clearly. When you lose vagueness, you become more available to your authentic self. Hence, dive in for distinctions. Are you really feeling okay or could you be somewhat melancholic? What's that tinge of sadness that's stopping you from feeling better about yourself? What's the story behind the sadness?

From the awareness of your true feelings comes new insight. From the insight comes preferred choices and conscious action. Like many other journalers, I find that I get to real substance after the first page and a half. Like pulling a curtain veil, truth gradually reveals.
"When we put the pen to paper, we articulate things in our life that we may have felt vague about. Before you write about something, somebody says, 'How do you

feel?' and you say, 'Oh, I feel okay.' Then you write about it, and you discover you don't feel okay." - Julia Cameron, The Artist's Way

See if this happens for you too.

Journal Starters

If you have trouble getting started, try using one of these journal starters:

If I let myself admit it, I feel

_____

If I could give myself permission, I would

_____

If I were true to myself, I would

_____

If I believed I deserved to have fun, I would

_____

No one but me knows that I

_____

If I didn't have to do it perfectly, I would

_____

I know that I am resisting

_____

Make up your own journal starters and put them on index cards for the next time you have trouble getting started.

4. Be In the Meditative Flow.

Meditative flow states are a clue to what feels satisfying to your soul. Allow God or a stream of consciousness to flow through you as you write. Your prayer invocation has set the stage and hence, being in the flow becomes easier.

Ms. Cameron describes the morning pages as "three pages of longhand writing, strictly stream-of-consciousness," done as soon as one wakes. They are "not meant to be art. Or even writing. They need not be smart, or funny, or particularly deep — in fact, it's better if they're not."

Once again, don't censure your writing. As my experience shows, *Consciousness speaks in broken English sometimes*. There is a certain rhythm that you tune into after you've begun to write for a while. I call this being in the "*Meditative Flow*".

5. Practice Mindfulness Journaling.

Mindfulness means that the mind is fully attending to what's happening, to what you're doing, to the space you're moving through.

It may seem easy to achieve, except that we so often veer from the matter at hand. Our mind takes flight, we lose touch with our body, and pretty soon we're engrossed in obsessive thoughts about something that just happened or fretting about the future. And that makes us anxious.

With mindfulness journaling, you are present to your thoughts and feelings. At the same time, you are like an observer to them. Hence, you are not caught up in the story or feeling "hot and bothered" because you are attached.

You are to observe your sensory experience in a non-attached manner. Observe your breathing, observe emotions, observe thoughts, and so on, without reacting to them. You become aware of the incessant chatter of the ego.

Through mindfulness journaling, you are gaining an outside perspective to your story. Mindfulness meditation helps you to center yourself. You learn to release the past or what no longer serves you. Gain a sense of balanced awareness or equanimity. This is the fodder of true change!

"Write fast, write everything, include everything, write from your feelings, write from your body." -Tristine Ranier

By simply observing, your senses gradually becomes brighter and sharper. It is possible to detect details that you've not perceived before. Everything starts to appear unusually vivid, rich and beautiful.

6. Be Guided by Body Wisdom

As you read through the journal prompts, pay particular attention to your body sensations. Make a note of the ones that tingle with excitement and the ones that make you uncomfortable. Pay attention to your body's signals. Dive right in as to what the sensations can mean. Some questions are going to lead to additional questions. Be prepared to follow your inner guidance in answering them.

"Here in this body are the sacred rivers: here are the sun and moon as well as all the pilgrimage places...I have not encountered another temple as blissful as my own body." Sahara

If you are going through some physical, emotional, or mental discomfort, stop fighting it. Simply observe. When you do so, the discomfort becomes a lot less or may even vanish.

Approach journaling with a sense of openness, play and curiosity. Your body is a sacred temple with answers. Explore its hallways of wisdom. There are many rooms that you can enter to explore.

7. Invite in Love

It is important that you invite in love when journaling. This means two things. First, practice all forms of self-love that is, acceptance, compassion, trust, respect, care, and forgiveness. If you need to delve more, read my book [Self-Love Secrets](#) on the various aspects of loving oneself. Second, invite Love to help guide you in your answers to the journal prompts.

The questions can be unsettling or discomforting. Also, the answers you make can sometimes make you feel angry, uncomfortable, or scared. For whatever reason, you may even be tempted to tear your journaling paper apart.

It's important that you practice grace during the writing process. Don't force yourself to come up with answers immediately. Simply surrender! Allow yourself to see, feel or sense your answers. Be patient and wait. Let Love or your Inner Guidance take over for the answers to come.

Invite in love when holding the space for healing and transformation to happen. Negative emotions are just offering your feedback. At times, emotions like anger, sadness, and fear are telling of what you may need to accept, confront, or change in your life. At other times, these same emotions might hint at people, places, or things you need to minimize or avoid so that you can keep safe.

Look out for thoughts that make you feel "bad", "wrong" or "imperfect". Tell yourself that they are not true. They are falsehoods that have crushed your spirit for a long time. It's time to align with the truth and love yourself for who you really are.

Be aware that you can only make a personal transformation, by first knowing and acknowledging where you are right now. Bathe yourself in mists of healing pink or green. Be gracious and give yourself a loving space. *Journaling serves as a tool for wisdom, in a gentle invitation for change.*

Chapter 3 – 50 Journal Prompts To Start for Self-Discovery

Finding yourself may sound like an inherently self-centered goal, but it is actually an unselfish process. In order to be a better partner, parent, friend or member of the society, it is important that you first know who you are, who you are not, what you value and what you have to offer.

Answering the following questions will not only lead you to discover more about yourself but also, guide you towards developing confidence and self-mastery. Reflecting is also key. Hence, spend time diving deeper for better answers.

"It takes courage....to endure the sharp pains of self-discovery rather than choose to take the dull pain of unconsciousness that would last the rest of our lives." Marianne Williamson

You may find that certain journal prompts in the book appear to be the same. Attempt them all anyway, on different days. I invite you to answer from a different angle or perspective or perhaps dive more deeply. Like me, you may just discover more gems.

Ready to go? Begin!

50 Journal Questions to Start

1. What do I like about myself?

   _____

   _____

   _____

   _____

2. What would I like to change about myself?

   _____

   _____

   _____

   _____

3. What do others say that they appreciate in me?

   _____

   _____

   _____

   _____

4. What are my strengths?

___

5. What are my most important values? How am I living in ways that are aligned with my values and how am I not?

___

6. What do I appreciate in myself?

___

7. Do I like what I look like? Why? Why not?

_____

_____

_____

_____

_____

8. Am I an action-taker or do I tend to procrastinate and why?

_____

_____

_____

_____

_____

9. Am I more positive or negative in my speech? What's my talk like? What can I change?

_____

_____

_____

_____

_____

10. Who inspires me? What qualities do these people have?

11. What do I fear the most and why?

12. How can I overcome my fears?

13. What do I love to do? What would I want to do?

_____

_____

_____

_____

_____

14. What makes me feel motivated, inspired, excited?

_____

_____

_____

_____

_____

15. What puts me in the flow?

_____

_____

_____

_____

_____

16. Am I physically healthy? In what ways am I healthy or unhealthy?

_____
_____
_____
_____
_____

17. Am I emotionally healthy? How am I healthy or unhealthy?

_____
_____
_____
_____
_____

18. Am I mentally healthy? In what ways am I healthy or unhealthy?

_____
_____
_____
_____
_____

19. Am I spiritually healthy? In what ways am I healthy or unhealthy?

_____

_____

_____

_____

_____

20. Do I laugh? Do I enjoy life? How can I feel more joyful?

_____

_____

_____

_____

_____

21. What are my most important values and how am I living in ways that are not aligned with my values?

_____

_____

_____

_____

_____

22. Which words describe me best? What's my personality like?

_____
_____
_____
_____
_____

23. What's one thing I would like to do more of and why? How can I make that happen?

_____
_____
_____
_____
_____

24. What's one thing I would like to do less of and why? How can I make that happen?

_____
_____
_____
_____
_____

25. What is a positive memory that stands out from childhood? What am I feeling as I recall it now?

26. What is a positive memory that stands out from adulthood? What am I feeling as I recall it now?

27. What is a negative memory that stands out from childhood? What has it taught me about myself?

28. What is a negative memory that stands out from adulthood? What has it taught me?

_____
_____
_____
_____
_____

29. What am I proud of achieving? What is my greatest achievement in my life?

_____
_____
_____
_____
_____

30. What are my most important needs and desires? Does my present life fulfill them?

_____
_____
_____
_____
_____

31. What are my spiritual beliefs like? How do I intend to grow spiritually? Name 3 ways.

_____

_____

_____

_____

_____

32. What does success mean to me? Do I see myself as successful? How do I measure success?

_____

_____

_____

_____

_____

33. How do I feel about the pace of my life? Is it too fast, too slow or just about right? What else can I do to create more balance?

_____

_____

_____

_____

_____

34. Do I surround myself with mostly positive or mostly negative people? How does that work for me?

_____
_____
_____
_____
_____

35. Do I trust my intuition? In what ways am I guided by it?

_____
_____
_____
_____
_____

36. How much do I trust myself? Do I listen to others more than myself?

_____
_____
_____
_____
_____

37. If I had all the time in the world, what would I want to do first?

38. What's draining my energy? How can I reduce or cut it out?

39. What are the rituals that I can adopt to start my day on a more positive note?

40. What does my ideal day look like? What can I do or change to align with this picture I have?

___

41. How do I feel about self-care and how does that effect the quality of my life?

___

42. Who means the world to me and why?

___

43. What lessons did I learn this week?

_____
_____
_____
_____
_____

44. What's the biggest lesson in my life that I've learned?

_____
_____
_____
_____
_____

45. If I could have one wish, it would be ...

_____
_____
_____
_____
_____

46. Am I an introvert or an extrovert? Am I energized being around others or being by myself?

_____
_____
_____
_____

47. I've just inherited $3 million. Now that money is less of an issue, what do I love to do with my life?

_____
_____
_____
_____

48. What can I do today that makes me feel rich (in spite of how much I have in my bank)?

_____
_____
_____
_____
_____

49. I know I'm stressed when ...

_____
_____
_____
_____

50. What's my biggest dream? How does the thought of achieving it make me feel?

_____
_____
_____
_____

Bonus Gifts

If you'd like to download the entire list of 250 journal questions and writing prompts for easy reference, as well as a list of 101 positive affirmations for your Divine Feminine, please claim them here at https://www.EvelynLim.com/claim-divine-feminine-gifts

Chapter 4 – 50 Journal Prompts for Your Inner Therapist

As mentioned, journaling is akin to having a therapist. Except that you are the one working on yourself. It's important you are able to step aside after writing down your thoughts to gain a clearer perspective.

When answering journal prompts, it may at first surprise you with the realization of what your inner talk has been saying. When you pay closer attention, you become aware of what your thoughts and emotions are like. Some of them may not be pretty. What's important is that you maintain non-judgment.

"What you have been saying to yourself comes from an inner voice. You had been having internal conversations about yourself, others and your stories about the world. Your self-talk exists at the mental level, which affects you emotionally." – Self-Love Secrets

I was in for a rude shock myself. In one revealing writing exercise, I found out that I was my worst enemy. As I have shared above in my Self-Love Secrets book, I had very dark moments where I turned against myself. Luckily, much has changed since then. These days, I'm able to apply a lot more empathy, love and compassion.

Journaling offers you a safe place to practice self-honesty. It is also a chance for you to undertake personal responsibility. Self-honesty in journaling makes it possible for you to process your negative perspective before you can refame your mind and to move forward!

Drink lots of calming green tea. Shut out noise as you attempt the next 50 journal prompts. Wrap yourself in a soft pink blanket. Clutch your teddy bear soft toy. Dose yourself with plenty of forgiveness if needed.

(Note: Should you have challenges with processing your answers after answering the questions below, do reach out to a trained professional. Contact me, if you need further assistance, at http://www.EvelynLim.com/contact.)

50 Journal Questions for Restoring Inner Balance

The following questions will help you to discover yourself psychologically…

1. What is something negative that I am feeling right now? As I think about it, do I allow myself to release the physical discomfort in my body?

2. What does my inner critic say when I look in the mirror?

3. Am I holding onto something that would be better to let go of? What is it and what's holding me back from letting go?

4. Do I have much control over my emotions? Why or why not?

_____
_____
_____
_____
_____

5. What is one memory that still bothers me today? What can I do to resolve it now?

_____
_____
_____
_____
_____

6. What is something I am ashamed of? How can I deal with this?

_____
_____
_____
_____
_____

7. When I'm in physical or emotional pain, what are some of the best things I can do for myself?

_____

_____

_____

_____

_____

8. What are my top 3 limiting beliefs that have impacted my life in undesirable ways? Are the beliefs still true for me today? What positive beliefs can I transform them to?

_____

_____

_____

_____

_____

9. What dramas in my life have I been addicted to? What are the recurring patterns like?

_____

_____

_____

_____

_____

10. What drains my energy? How can I remove it from my life or protect myself from its negative effect?

_____
_____
_____
_____
_____

11. What's keeping me awake at night? How can I resolve this?

_____
_____
_____
_____
_____

12. How do I feel about my last mistake and what did I learn from it?

_____
_____
_____
_____
_____

13. What's my biggest worry right now? How do I intend to overcome it? What are the strategies that I can employ?

_____
_____
_____
_____
_____

14. What's my biggest frustration right now? How do I intend to overcome it?

_____
_____
_____
_____
_____

15. How do I usually move past unpleasant thoughts or experiences? What are ways that I can improve on letting go of things that no longer serve me?

_____
_____
_____
_____
_____

16. Do I have unfinished business? With whom? What inner work needs to be done to heal this? What steps can I take to bring resolution?

_____
_____
_____
_____
_____

17. On a scale of 1 - 10, where am I when it comes to being calm and centered in challenging situations? What do I need to do to have more peace in my life?

_____
_____
_____
_____
_____

18. In what areas of my life am I trading authenticity for safety, or what appears to be safety?

_____
_____
_____
_____
_____

19. What holds me back from being more authentic?

20. How do I feel when I enforce my personal boundaries? Is there anything that I need to change with enforcing this?

21. How do I sabotage myself?

22. In what ways do I feel responsible for everyone and everything?

_____
_____
_____
_____
_____

23. What are some of the limiting beliefs about money and being rich that I have? Can I transform these to more empowering ones? If so, what would these be?

_____
_____
_____
_____
_____

24. Is my self-acceptance conditional, dependent upon the validation of others or specific accomplishments? If so, in what ways?

_____
_____
_____
_____
_____

25. Do I hold back from asking the big questions? The hard questions? If so, what scares me?

26. How do I hesitate or refuse to take action on what my heart tells me?

27. Whenever I felt bothered by someone or something negatively, what are my usual immediate reactions?

28. How do I cultivate more compassion?

_____
_____
_____
_____

29. How do I cultivate more self-love or the feeling that I am good enough?

_____
_____
_____
_____

30. How do I cultivate more patience and understanding?

_____
_____
_____
_____

31. If I can change one thing in my life, what would I change and why?

32. Where does my pain originate? What would need to happen for me to heal?

33. List three specific situations and/or times when I was most happy in my life. What factors were present when I felt that way? How was I feeling about myself during those times?

34. What do I fear most in my life right now? Why? What would it mean if that happened?

_____

_____

_____

_____

_____

35. When do I feel the most angry or frustrated? What is it about those situations that I feel that way?

_____

_____

_____

_____

_____

36. What are my favorite ways to take care of myself physically, emotionally, mentally, and spiritually?

_____

_____

_____

_____

_____

37. Do I have any regrets about my life so far? What changes can I make so I don't continue to live with regrets?

_____
_____
_____
_____
_____

38. What does vulnerability mean to me? How can I show up, by embracing who I am, with a lot more courage?

_____
_____
_____
_____
_____

39. What does my inner critic tell me? How does it stop me from moving forward?

_____
_____
_____
_____
_____

40. What important needs do I have that aren't getting met?

_____
_____
_____
_____
_____

41. As I think about my stress right now, my body is having some reactions. What are the reactions like? What can I do to release them?

_____
_____
_____
_____
_____

42. What advice would I give to my 5-year old younger self? (Do I follow this advice now?)

_____
_____
_____
_____
_____

43. What makes me come alive? When was the last time I felt truly alive?

___

44. How do I know if something makes me feel good? What are my body sensations like?

___

45. What are my primary beliefs about love? (it's easy, scary, short-lived, feels good, not possible, difficult, etc.) Where/when did I acquire those beliefs? Do I still believe them? Why or why not?

___

46. What does my ego self say about me? What does my spiritual self have to say to my ego self? Alternatively, what wise advice can my spiritual self give to my ego self?

_____
_____
_____
_____

47. What emotions do I want to feel most of the time? What would I like to feel most of the time?

_____
_____
_____
_____

48. What 3 positive affirmations can I make for centering myself today?

_____
_____
_____
_____

49. How do I feel and respond when I fail?

___

50. What brings me emotional peace?

___

Chapter 5 – 60 Journal Prompts for Connecting with Your Sacred Feminine Power

This chapter is designed to awaken your Sacred Feminine Power and take you deeper into self-inquiry. If you are new to connecting with your innate nature, practice patience. It helps!

"I was once afraid of people saying "Who does she think she is? Now I have the courage to stand and say, "This is who I am." Oprah Winfrey

Connecting with your Divine Feminine requires you to be vulnerable. Courage is required. You agree to be vulnerable, raw in your writings. Instead of struggling to put on false appearances and feeling fearful of being rejected, you can be honest with yourself. There is no need for you to conform to the standards held by any masculine-led community. And it is safe for you to express your true thoughts on your journal pages.

In fact, Brene Brown, research professor at the University of Houston and one of my favorite authors, says, there is power in vulnerability.

"Vulnerability is the birthplace of love, belonging, joy, courage, empathy, and creativity. It is the source of hope, empathy, accountability, and authenticity. If we want greater clarity in our purpose or deeper and more meaningful spiritual lives, vulnerability is the path." – Brené Brown

If you stay with the journaling process, you will find vulnerability giving way to quiet strength. It is a strength that you can trust. By trusting yourself more, you are likely to find a better connection with your intuition.

A better connection brings about greater confidence. It's certainly what I had found for myself. When I don't have a logical reasoning behind some of the decsions that my husband and I need to make, I'd yell out to him, "Just trust me!"

Clarissa Pinkola Estés, author of Women Who Run With the Wolves: Myths and Stories of the Wild Woman Archetype, has this to say about intuition...

"Practice listening to your intuition, your inner voice; ask questions; be curious; see what you see; hear what you hear, and then act upon what you know to be true. These intuitive powers were given to your soul at birth."
Clarissa Pinkola Estés

To discover more about your innate qualities, you can explore archetypal patterns of the feminine energy. According to Jungian psychology, an archetype is a collectively-inherited unconscious idea, pattern of thought, image, etc., that is universally present, in individual psyches. One of archetypal patterns relating to the feminine archetype that is easy to understand is the Mother.

The Creator Mother within the soul of a Divine Feminine is like Earth. She has maternal instincts which makes her very caring. As a Mother, she nourishes us with milk and she keeps us alive. Through her womb, a mother allows the merging of the masculine and feminine energy for creation to happen. She is akin to a Midwife, facilitating birth.

The Divine Feminine is a Healer, whose loving and caring nature helps to heal relationships. Her innate nature is full of grace. She is connected to water for emotional management.

The Divine Feminine is sensous. Sensuality is the ability to fully experience the senses, without apology or restraint. The sense of smell, taste, touch, and vision combine to awaken her body. *The Divine Feminine honors her sacred body temple with unconditional love. She is also a Sensual Lover who unites her energy with her masculine partner as ONE.*

The Divine Feminine understands that even as her body ages, she does not need to resort to invasive procedures to keep her youth. Nor does she need to fear losing her man because she is older. She has enough self-confidence to know that she is still beautiful. Her graceful nature reveals itself with age.

"The beauty in a woman is not in the clothes she wears, the figure that she carries, or the way she combs her hair. The beauty of a woman is seen in her eyes because that is the doorway to her heart; the place where love resides. True beauty in a woman is reflected in her soul. It's the caring and that she lovingly gives the passion that she shows and the beauty of a woman only grows with passing years." - Audrey Hepburn

Connecting with your Feminine Energy requires you to listen to body wisdom. Your body is wise. It offers you feedback and is a vessel for change to happen. You can choose to engage your body wisdom through the chakra system. I will be offering some guidance on how you can do so in a later section.

The Divine Feminine is a Wise Sage, using her intuition to guide her for decision making. She senses energy, whether consciously or unconsciously, and is able to tell if something feels off or not right. In a state of balance, she is calm and therefore, not a chronic worrier but a Warrioress. As a Warriorress, she is able to deal with challenges and gets things done.

Creativity is the signature of the Divine Feminine. She is very linked to arts such as painting, music, and photography. Her creativity can help her to carve out unique work for herself. Thus, she does not need to be in a co-dependent relationship.

Most certainly, the modern woman does not have to rely on her partner to create a source of living. She has what it takes to succeed. Success is hers when she deems herself worthy. For navigating life, she is guided by personal truth and intuition.

"We will discover the nature of our particular genius when we stop trying to conform to our own or to other people's models, learn to be ourselves, and allow our natural channel to open." Shakti Gawain

If all these sound like Greek to you, don't worry! It's more important that you get the journal writing going. Do the exercises with open curiosity and see what comes up for you.

Prepare as you would for meditation. Go quiet. Invoke the prayer, if you want to. Read the question for the day. Wait a bit. Tune in and allow answers or messages to emerge. Let your fingers do the writing.

53 Journal Questions for Embracing Your Divine Feminine

1. Describe my feminine superpower. What are the words that I can use to celebrate myself?

_____

_____

_____

_____

_____

2. What gifts, talents, and passions have I been hiding from myself and the world? What can I do to start engaging with them?

_____

_____

_____

_____

_____

3. The Nurturing Mother in me loves to...

_____

_____

_____

_____

4. The Divine Warrioress in me has these feminine qualities that help me deal with challenges. They are.....

_____
_____
_____
_____

5. How can I align with the feminine qualities or attributes that can help me manifest what I want?

_____
_____
_____
_____

6. What's my archetypal pattern as a Sensual Lover like? What's coming up for me as I tune into my body?

_____
_____
_____
_____

7. Do I honor and love my feminine side? Do I honor and love my masculine side? How do I draw on both to navigate life changes?

_____
_____
_____
_____

8. Does my Divine Feminine need healing? What's stopping her (or me) from the full expression of her (my) divinity?

_____
_____
_____
_____

9. On a scale of 1 to 10, how much do I honor, love and respect my body? In what ways am I honoring, loving and respecting my body and in what ways I'm not?

_____
_____
_____
_____

10. What 3 positive affirmations can I say to myself for accessing my Divine Feminine?

11. Which Sacred Goddess, Goddesses or Spiritual Feminine Energy do I feel aligned with and why?

12. What limiting beliefs about being a woman that I need to let go of? What are the opposite positive beliefs that I need to make for accessing my feminine power instead?

13. What are the ways that I can nurture myself so that I can absolutely shine my Feminine Power?

14. What is my heart or intuition saying to me today?

15. How can I show up more fully today?

16. My Divine Feminine has this message for me today…

17. What does my "thank you" letter to Mother Earth say?

18. What message does Mother Earth have for me today?

19. Which female role model inspires me and why?

_____

_____

_____

_____

20. How can I celebrate myself even as I age?

_____

_____

_____

_____

21. What are my thoughts on aging like? Do I need to change any of these?

_____

_____

_____

_____

22. What is my mantra for living in fullness like?

23. How can I center myself today?

24. What would put me in the flow that brings out the best in me?

25. Are dominating male characters there in my life? What are my personal boundary guidelines that I have? How do I want to be treated by others especially the males in my life?

_____
_____
_____
_____
_____

26. Do I tend to play the victim? Do I give myself the permission to let the story of victimhood go?

_____
_____
_____
_____
_____

27. What beliefs have I inherited from my parents and grandparents that no longer serve me today? What can I do to overcome them?

_____
_____
_____
_____
_____

28. What beauty do I see in the world today?

29. If I wasn't afraid, I would ...

30. In what areas of my life am I underestimating myself with my excuses and why?

31. How can I invite in grace today?

_____

_____

_____

_____

_____

32. What untruths can I empty out today?

_____

_____

_____

_____

_____

33. My Inner Sage has this message for me today....

_____

_____

_____

_____

_____

34. What is my passion? What fires my soul?

_____
_____
_____
_____

35. In what ways am I excusing myself from living my best life? Am I drinking or shopping to excess?

_____
_____
_____
_____

36. What's my relationship with food like?

_____
_____
_____
_____

37. What's my relationship with money like? Do I perceive myself as less capable of handling money as compared to men?

_____
_____
_____
_____

38. What drives my choices in life – love or fear?

_____
_____
_____
_____

39. In what ways can I stop craving the approval of others?

_____
_____
_____
_____

40. What's the emotional story behind the physical part of my body that needs healing?

41. What are my secret wildest fantasies?

42. Am I often prone to jealousy or envy of other women? In what ways, can I let this go?

43. Do I find myself leaning on men to make decisions? What's my decision-making process like?

_____
_____
_____
_____
_____

44. What are 3 promises that I can keep to myself? State them now.

_____
_____
_____
_____
_____

45. What creative activity can I undertake for this week?

_____
_____
_____
_____
_____

46. What are the things that I can declutter from my closet or home this week?

_____
_____
_____
_____
_____

47. What are my addictions? Do I allow myself to give them up?

_____
_____
_____
_____
_____

48. How can I unleash my creative genius?

_____
_____
_____
_____
_____

49. Do I apply my intuition for decision making? What's my intuition superpower like?

50. How can I channel my sensuality and attractiveness today?

51. How can I celebrate my connection with Mother Earth today?

52. In what ways can I support or make a difference to other women in the world?

53. What self-care activity or activities can I undertake to support my Divine Feminine today?

7 Questions For Connecting with Your Chakras

Heard of the chakra system? Working with your chakras and balancing them can help you with benefits such as improving your emotional states and for self-discovery.

I am giving you a quick overview so that you can use the journal prompts that are related to chakras in this section. Chakra is a Sanksrit word meaning "wheel" or "circle". The entire Chakra system is a complex network of energy channels connecting the wheels and is mapped throughout the whole body.

There are 7 major Chakra energy centers. They are found running alongside the spine. Here's a picture of the chakra system...

The Chakra System
- Seventh or Crown Chakra
- Sixth or Third Eye Chakra
- Fifth or Throat Chakra
- Fourth or Heart Chakra
- Third or Solar Plexus Chakra
- Second or Sacral Chakra
- First or Root Chakra

Each chakra is said to vibrate at a different frequency and is associated with a color. It is also associated with certain emotions and organs and their function.

First or Root Chakra

Your root chakra is located at the base or root, the perineum. This chakra represents grounding, and survival needs like shelter and security. If you find yourself scattered and have difficulty with centering yourself, this is the chakra that you need to work on.

Location: Base of spine in tailbone area.
Responsible for: Survival issues such as financial independence, money, and food.
Color: Red
Body organs: Spinal column, the kidneys, legs, and colon.

Second or Sacral Chakra

Its location is indicative two to three inches below the navel and in. This chakra represents pleasure, emotional balance, and sexuality. If you have problems with manifesting, giving birth to a child, or creating healthy one-on-one relationships with another, you will need to heal this chakra.

Location: Lower abdomen.
Responsible for: Reproduction, fertility, pleasure, sexuality, addictions, and manifestation.
Color: Orange
Body organs: Reproductive organs and bladder.

Third or Solar Plexus Chakra

Located by the belly button, this chakra represents your willpower and assertion. It governs your self-esteem and your beliefs on whether you are good enough or not. Hence, if you don't believe that you are "good enough", this is the chakra to work on.

Location: Upper abdomen in the stomach area.
Responsible for: Self-esteem and confidence.
Color: Yellow
Body organs: pancreas, liver, and stomach.

Fourth or Heart Chakra

Located centrally around and above the heart, this chakra represents unconditional love, acceptance, and compassion. A block in your heart-chakra makes it hard for you to practice self-love, love for others and forgiveness.

Location: Center of chest just above the heart.

Responsible for: Love, joy, and relationships with others.
Color: Pink or Green
Body organs: Heart and your circulatory system.

Fifth or Throat Chakra

Located at the throat, this chakra is all about communication, creativity, and reliability. It is about your ability to express yourself and the stand for truth. If you are blocked in your fith or throat chakra, you will face difficulty with expression.

Location: Throat.
Responsible for: Communication, self-expression of truth.
Color: blue

Body organs: Thyroid, hypothalamus, throat, and mouth.

Sixth or Third Eye Chakra

Located between the eyes on your forehead, this chakra is often associated with your psychic or sixth sense. It represents your ability to connect with intuition, imagination, and wisdom. Hence, if you are feeling blocked in these areas, this is the chakra to work on.

Location: forehead between the eyes.
Responsible for: Intuition, imagination, and wisdom.
Color: Deep purple
Body organs: Pituitary gland, the nose, the ears, and the pineal gland.

Seventh or Crown Chakra

The only chakra to be found located just above the crown of the head in what is considered your "spiritual body". This chakra is associated with spiritual consciousness and a higher state of being. A block in the seventh or crown chakra leads to spiritual disconnection.

Location: The very top of the head.
Responsible for: Spiritual connection and pure bliss.
Color: Light purple or indigo.
Body organs: Above top of the head.

How to Work with Our Chakras

Get an understanding of each chakra center and then,

work on the journal prompt associated with each chakra center. Before you begin to journal, follow the steps

- refer to the chakra picture to know which part you are working on
- visualize yourself being bathed in the energy of the color that is associated with the chakra
- place attention on its location on your body
- stay present to the awareness of the color, location, and sensations that arise.

1. What message does my first root chakra have for me today?

_____

_____

_____

_____

_____

2. What message does my sacral chakra have for me today?

_____

_____

_____

_____

_____

3. What message does my solar plexus chakra have for me today?

_____
_____
_____
_____

4. What message does my heart chakra have for me today?

_____
_____
_____
_____

5. What message does my throat chakra have for me today?

_____
_____
_____
_____

6. What message does my third eye have for me today?

_____
_____
_____
_____
_____

7. What message does my crown chakra have for me today?

_____
_____
_____
_____
_____

Bonus Gift

Would you like a list of 101 positive affirmations that helps you with supporting your Divine Feminine? Fill out your details when you click over the link below, so that I can send you the download...

https://www.EvelynLim.com/claim-divine-feminine-gifts

Chapter 5 – 50 Journal Prompts for Knowing Yourself Via Relationships

The relationships that you have with others can indirectly tell you more about yourself, the way you think and feel and your aspirations. In relating to others, adopt the view that everyone can be a teacher for you. Your responses and reactions to your relationships provide valuable feedback on how you can make changes.

In the questions below, you are also asked to examine your relationships with your partner, your children, parents, and your friends. Reflect on the quality of your relationships. I recommend using the opportunity to do gratitude exercises. Express your gratitude to loved ones. Bring attention to how blessed you are to have them in your life. Gratitude exercises will help bring about closeness and greater connection.

"Gratitude makes sense of our past, brings peace for today, and creates a vision for tomorrow." – Melody Beattie

Granted, not everyone is going to feel blessed. It may be that you were traumatized by your parents as a child or by your spouse. For such situations, think about how you can reframe your perspective, so that you are no longer held hostage by past grievances.

Finally, working through challenges that you have with them helps you to strengthen and grow. An awareness of how you can improve the relationships that you have puts you in good stead with your loved ones. *The Divine*

Feminine desires authentic connection, trust, and intimacy. This desire is innate in you.

50 Journal Questions on Relationships

If you are currently single and looking for an ideal partner

1. What specific attributes do I want my ideal life partner to possess?

2. Am I expecting a Prince Charming to come rescue me? If so, why or why not?

3. What's the vision I have in terms of an ideal relationship?

If you are currently in a marriage/life partnership/relationship that you would like to work on...

4. Who am I and what am I like when I am with this person?

_____
_____
_____
_____
_____

5. If currently in a marriage/life/relationship, am I happy? Why or why not?

_____
_____
_____
_____
_____

6. What is the biggest challenge I see in the relationship?

_____
_____
_____
_____

7. Am I expecting my spouse to be the "provider" for the family? Is this expectation causing any issue?

8. What is the One thing that I can do to bring the relationship to the next level immediately?

9. What did I appreciate about this person when I first met him/her?

10. What do I appreciate about my partner now? Specify at least 3 qualities.

_____
_____
_____
_____
_____

11. What were the past relationship hurts that I hold on to? What do I need to let go of?

_____
_____
_____
_____
_____

12. What is the single biggest belief change I could make that would improve my relationship?

_____
_____
_____
_____
_____

13. What's the vision that I hold for us in 10 year's time?

_____
_____
_____
_____

14. How can I introduce more love into my relationship?

_____
_____
_____
_____

15. In what ways can I show up as a great partner working together to weather any storm or challenges?

_____
_____
_____
_____

16. Whenever I feel irritated by my spouse, I know that he or she is triggering something that I think and feel about myself. What is it?

_____
_____
_____
_____

17. If there is a 14-day romantic getaway that we can go to, where would I like this place to be and why?

_____
_____
_____
_____

18. If I am to write a letter to express thanks to my partner, I would say...

_____
_____
_____
_____

19. I ask forgiveness from my partner for.....

_____
_____
_____
_____
_____

20. What would a great level-10 relationship look like?

_____
_____
_____
_____
_____

In your relationships with your children...

21. What can I celebrate about when I think about my relationship with my child or children?

_____
_____
_____
_____
_____

22. My love letter to one of my children reads like this...

_____

_____

_____

_____

_____

23. Here's what I feel like saying to my child as a form of advice....

_____

_____

_____

_____

_____

24. I am thankful to my children for...

_____

_____

_____

_____

_____

25. I ask for forgiveness from my children for...

_____
_____
_____
_____

26. How I would like to improve my relationship with my children...

_____
_____
_____
_____

27. When I think about my children, I feel...

_____
_____
_____
_____

28. I would like to inspire my children to...

_____
_____
_____
_____

29. The values that I would like my children to learn are...

_____
_____
_____
_____

30. My motivational "don't give up" speech to my children is...

_____
_____
_____
_____

In your relationship with parents...

31. How's my relationship with my parents like? From a scale of 1-10, how do I rate my relationship with them?

_____
_____
_____
_____
_____

32. When I think about my parents, I think and feel...

_____
_____
_____
_____
_____

33. My gratitude letter to my parents goes like this....

_____
_____
_____
_____
_____

34. I would like to ask forgiveness from them....

35. My happiest memory when I was a child with them is...

36. My happiest memory as an adult with them is...

37. To heal my relationship with them, I intend to let go of...

___

38. What are the things that I can do to show that I care about them this week?

___

39. If I can tell my parent (whether mum or dad) what I truly think and feel, I would say....

___

40. What I would like to celebrate about my dad is....

_____

_____

_____

_____

_____

41. What I would like to celebrate about my mum is....

_____

_____

_____

_____

_____

42. The best things that they have taught me are...

_____

_____

_____

_____

_____

In your relationships with friends...

43. What friends do I enjoy spending time with? What are their qualities like?

___

44. My "thank you" letter to my close friend goes like this...

___

45. What do my friends describe about me? What do they value in me?

___

46. In times of trouble, who can I count on and why?

47. How can I channel more love into my friendships?

48. Who can I forgive whom I feel has wronged me? Write a forgiveness letter to this person.

49. What are my views about toxic relationships? Am I in any right now? If so, how can I move away from these relationships and invest in the more supportive ones?

_____

_____

_____

_____

_____

50. What are my thoughts on friendships? What are my thoughts on having male and female friends?

_____

_____

_____

_____

_____

Chapter 6 – 20 Journal Questions for Knowing Yourself Via Work Life

Your work life can tell you more about yourself. It may be that you've been so caught up in the busyness of the caffeinated world, that you did not make time for taking stock. Saying "yes" to journaling can change this.

Using the journal prompts, you'd be asked to reflect on the current situation and what changes, if any, you'd like to experience. Are you focusing on the things that matter? And also, what can you do to improve your overall well-being?

The Divine Feminine has a dream that she may like to pursue when it comes to work. She is not meant to stay hidden in the kitchen if she so chooses. She can achieve a lot more than just doing the laundry, taking care of babies or washing dirty dishes. In the office or at work, she contributes value. The Divine Feminine is bright, diligent and has the willingness to learn.

"Courage belongs to the woman who knows herself and who decides to go for her dreams."

Connecting with Sacred Feminine Power allows you to access what she truly wants while balancing family needs. It helps to establish your confidence and to assert financial independence. Meet her and maximize your work potential with the following set of questions.

20 Journal Questions about Work Life

1. What work would I love to do? Am I doing the work that I love now?

2. What are my thoughts on creating work-life balance and how am I accomplishing this right now?

3. What's the ONE thought that I can change now that can help bring about a breakthrough at work?

4. What qualities, strengths and talents do I have that helps me create my best work?

___

5. What is the one word that describes the value that I bring to the world through my work?

___

6. What life lessons has my work life taught me?

___

7. How did I spend my week at work? Did I feel accomplished, happy, disappointed, frustrated, etc?

_____
_____
_____
_____
_____

8. What's my ideal job like?

_____
_____
_____
_____
_____

9. What's an ideal day at work like?

_____
_____
_____
_____
_____

10. Where do I see myself work-wise one year from now?

11. How do I see myself work-wise three years from now?

12. What should I be prioritizing for work right now? Am I working on my priorities?

13. What are the tasks that I can delegate out to others, as they do not fit into my strengths?

_____
_____
_____
_____
_____

14. What is the next thing that I can learn, in order to help me improve my results in the next 3 to 6 months?

_____
_____
_____
_____
_____

15. What can I do to improve my well-being at work?

_____
_____
_____
_____
_____

16. What kind of work environment best supports my wellness and growth?

17. What is my ideal office like? Where is this office?

18. What type of clients would I like to work with and attract?

19. What type of colleagues, work partners or team players would I like to work with and attract?

___

20. If I am to introduce myself and tell someone what I do, I'd say…

___

Chapter 7 – 20 Journal Questions for Aligning with Purpose & Spiritual Consciousness

If you have been going around feeling empty and if you find that your life has no meaning, you may want to ask yourself what your purpose in life is. Knowing why you are here and how you would like to impact others is going to make you feel a lot more fulfilled. *You feel fulfilled when you align with purpose.*

"Learn to get in touch with the silence within yourself and know that everything in this life has a purpose." Elizabeth Kubler Ross

Mediocrity happens by default. You've been given roadmaps that follow a conventional path in life that it may not have occurred to you to ask deeper questions. If you are getting by or even doing well, you may not have felt the need to question. Not until you hit the moment when you realize that you've been asleep all this while.

As Socrates once said, the unexamined life is not worth living. You certainly wouldn't want to wait till the end of your life, to begin asking questions. Also, may I suggest that in order to get clearer answers, you need to ask better questions. Don't procrastinate any longer. Answer the following journaling prompts to start reflecting!

20 Journal Questions on Purpose & Spiritual Consciousness

1. What's my higher purpose in life? In other words, what's the difference I am hoping to make?

_____
_____
_____
_____
_____

2. What's the vision I have for the world?

_____
_____
_____
_____
_____

3. What's my mantra or manifesto for magical living like?

_____
_____
_____
_____
_____

4. What delusions do I need to remove, in order to know who I am?

___

5. Three years from now, my life is going to look like this...

___

6. Ten years from now, my life is going to look like this...

___

7. What's the legacy I hope to create?

___

8. When my partner or loved one reads out my eulogy at my funeral, it will say the following...

___

9. What would my 80-year old self say to me right now?

___

10. What does my future self who's living in full potential look like?

11. To someone who is awakening, I would say this...

12. What fairy tale, folklore or ancient story that essentially describes the archetypal story of my life? Could this be my pain to power story?

13. If I only have 6 months left to live, would I change the way I am living my life now? What do I change?

_____
_____
_____
_____
_____

14. If I can go back 5 years, what would I change? What can I do now?

_____
_____
_____
_____
_____

15. Who (or what) is God or pure consciousness?

_____
_____
_____
_____
_____

16. What are my beliefs on spirituality or the power of the Universe?

_____
_____
_____
_____

17. If I allow myself to see what I am not seeing before, I would realize that....

_____
_____
_____
_____

18. What do I not only want...but what does my deepest self desire?

_____
_____
_____
_____

19. If I allow myself to be free, what will I discover?

20. If I take away all my identifications like my name, achievements, and labels, who am I?

Chapter 8 – Journaling Review

Did you accomplish your journaling objectives?

What are the messages that you have gained?

What are the lessons that you've learned?

How can you improve now?

To fully maximize your journaling experience, it is important that you do a review. Reviews are also opportunities for you to discover more about yourself. Adopting a growth mindset, with a willingness to learn and grow, when doing reviews is key.

"There is more to myself than anyone has so far discovered." Anonymous

Reviews help you to track your progress and how much you've gained from the start.

There are 3 levels of reviews that you can conduct:
1. Review your objectives
2. Review your answers
3. Review your journaling experience.

Review Your Objectives

What was your intended objective when you started to journal? Check back and see what you've written. Did you manage to achieve your objectives? If yes, great! I am happy for you. If not, are there questions that you could have asked yourself? Successful people ask better questions and as a result, they get better answers.

My journal prompts are meant to be a guide. They may not cover every situation. However, they are aimed to help you have an idea on how to frame questions and to get started on posting. Follow the guidance of your inner voice, while holding your intended objective at the back of your mind. See where that leads you.

Review What You Have Written

When reviewing what you have written, you are not censuring yourself. Instead, you are noticing consistent patterns.

How often are you using negative than positive statements?

Are you thinking and feeling more negative or positive most of the time?

Are you more of a heart or head person?

Are your journals filled with 4-letter words?

You are observing very closely the words that you have used. Look for distinctions. In other words, dive another layer to ask what your answer means to you.

Do you like yourself?

What about love?

Would you say "love" is a better word for the way you feel about yourself?

If not, would you like to feel love for yourself?

You are constantly asking yourself how you can reach for a better-feeling thought.

Can you turn your anger into peace and forgiveness?

Instead of focusing on the things that go wrong, can you direct your attention to more positive ones?

The more open you are to self-inqiry, the greater the opportunity for true clarity to emerge. You get better answers, which helps you create change. Little shifts lead to massive results.

If you need further assistance with emotional healing and restoring inner balance, do look for a trained coach or healing therapist. My speciality is in helping women release their resistances, rewrite their past and reset their vision. For more information on my services, feel free to check my site http://www.EvelynLim.com.

Reviewing Your Journaling Experience

What was it like for you when you first started journaling?

Was it hard for you to express yourself? What about after a week?

How long were you able to write for without interruption?

Was it easy for you to get into the meditative flow?

How can you improve your journaling experience?

Review how you've grown in your journaling experience. At the same time, notice if you have reduced your stress levels, feel more grateful, and become more aware and confident. Such are some of the benefits that you can potentially gain from your journaling journey!

Chapter 9 - Lessons for the Divine Feminine

In this chapter, I am laying out some lessons that you can potentially learn from connecting with the Divine Feminine. They are certainly what I have gathered from walking my path. These gems can act as triggers for deeper reflection as you review your journal answers.

"It's a perfect moment to quietly meditate on the cosmic Great Mother who can inspire us all; the divine, feminine Spirit of nurturance known as The Goddess, so revered in ancient times and being rediscovered by women today." - Sarah Ban Breathnach

Creative Power

Have you already realized how powerful you are? You have the ability to bring about magic. As a woman, you are biologically equipped for creation. It is only with your participation that evolution can happen.

Hence, you are to become aware of your birthright. You have a place in this world. Confidence comes from knowing that you are as worthy as anyone else on this planet. You deserve to be loved, respected, honored and celebrated.

As you connect with your energy, you are receptive. Your heart becomes open. Your gift is in bringing about healing of the divine masculine, and yet maintaining your freedom and independence.

"There is a vitality, a life force, an energy, a quickening,

that is translated through you into action, and because there is only one of you in all time, this expression is unique. And if you block it, it will never exist through any other medium and will be lost." Martha Graham

To align with your Divine Feminine, connect with Mother Earth and be in the flow. Go out in nature, take a walk barefoot and stand firm like a tree. Dance in the wind. Celebrate your being. Appreciate beauty everywhere. Do what you love, unleash your creativity and listen in to your heart. Undertake self-love at all levels.

Cosmic Womb

Through your womb, you will discover the interconnectedness that you have with others. Everyone comes from the same source. It's the Cosmic Womb that births every human. In the same manner, every living thing goes through the cycle of birth and death.

At the same time, while each of us are made up of the same essence, we are birthed with a unique blueprint. We are led to expressing ourselves in various ways. Some of us prefer to sing and some prefer to dance. All are equally valid.

"I have no sense of nationalism, only a cosmic consciousness of belonging to the human family." Rosika Schwimmer

While there is uniqueness, there is also unity, therefore. You celebrate humanity for all its diversity and oneness. You also hold life with a lot more reverence and appreciation of its beauty.

The Integration of Masculine and Feminine Energies

Have you ever come across the yin-yang symbol? The symbol comprises of a white and a black swirl. If you look carefully, there is black within the white swirl and white in the black swirl.

According to the Chinese philosophy, yin represents feminine energy and yang represents masculine energy. The yin-yang theory explains the nature of the universe in terms of these two opposing but complementary and interdependent forces. Yin-yang, masculine and feminine, is the energy of a whole being expressing itself.

"All things carry yin and embrace yang. They reach harmony by blending with the vital breath." - Laozi

Whether you are male or female, it is contained within you. Because you were born out of sexual energy – the meeting of a male and female – you carry both energies within you. Indeed, suppressing one side is not going to help you in terms of overall well-being. Neither does it do you any good to shame masculine energy, when you also have it too.

Do know that masculine energy is about domination and control only if the male ego is in charge. Otherwise, there are positive traits associated with masculine energy as much as there are with feminine energy. Both need to work together.

Ultimately, it's about reclaiming your wholeness so that you can live fully. Learn to honor both sides of you. *Put on your Invisible Crown and SHINE!*

Conclusion – Journaling for Sacred Self-Discovery

I believe that journaling can benefit everyone. It's why I had written this book. To recap, the following are the benefits that you can potentially derive from journaling:

Benefits of Journaling

1. *Journaling helps you in self-discovery and to foster spiritual growth.* You get to know more about yourself, who you are and who you are not. Through journal prompts, you are invited to reflect on questions that you don't normally think of on a daily basis. You are also asked to trust your intuition and be open to allow for answers to arise. It's a holistic activity that engages all parts of you – the emotional, mental, your body wisdom and the spiritual.

2. *Journaling is your invisible therapist, providing you with an opportunity to process your thoughts and feelings thus reducing stress.* It's how you can nurture your inner self and gives the suppressed part of yourself a chance to speak freely and safely. Detailing your thoughts and feelings with regards to a stressful event can be pretty much therapeutic. You are invited to release past hurts. Journaling brings about inner peace and harmony.

3. *Journaling helps you become a more effective communicator.* By articulating your thoughts and emotions in writing, you gain the potential to become a better communicator in your relationships. You are no longer vague or play the avoidance card because you have not processed your inner world. Instead, words

come more easily with balanced awareness. It potentially helps you to strengthen your relationships.

4. *Journaling helps you with greater confidence and boosts your self-esteem.* With increased understanding of yourself, you gain confidence. The exercise strengthens your core, providing a balance to external influences.

5. *Journaling helps to clear up cluttered thinking.* When you are too much in the head, you are unable to think clearly. Journaling offers you a way to get your thoughts out onto paper. As you review them on paper, you will find it a lot easier to come up with solutions.

6. *Journaling leads you to connect with your inner guidance.* You will become much more aware of the beliefs and sabotage patterns that slows your progress, growth, and results. Through journaling your answers, you are asking your inner guidance on how you can make a shift.

7. *Journaling helps you with gratitude and positive thinking.* You can use journaling as way to help you focus on areas of life that you'd like to place attention on. One example is to do gratitude journaling. With gratitude journaling, you are expressing thanks for the blessings that you experience in your life. It's uplifting for your soul!

8. *Journaling helps you create a vision of your ideal life and potentially connects you with purpose.* Through journal prompts, you prioritize what is important to you. You create a vision based on core ideals that inspires you to take aligned actions.

9. *Journaling aids in mindfulness meditation.* If you are having a hard time meditating on a cushion because your mind can't keep still, try journaling for a start. Journaling invites you to go into a quiet space and be present with your thoughts and emotions, as an observer. Mindfulness journaling ultimately helps you reduce anxiety and stress.

10. *Journaling helps to support your health and well-being.* Journaling benefits have been scientifically proven. Research shows that journaling
- decreases the symptoms of asthma, arthritis, and other health conditions
- improves cognitive functioning
- boost immune cell activity
- reduce viral load in AIDS patients
- speed up healing after surgery.

It's amazing how a simple technique can bring about huge payoffs. Here's my one-line description that sums up all of the above...

"Journaling is a low or no-cost writing therapy tool that can help you transform your life in the mind, body and spirit, and from the inside-out."

Journaling: The Way for Spiritual Transformation

I have told countless stories in my journal papers. They have helped me overcome anxiety and depression. During the course of writing, I was able to access greater joy, fufillment and creativity. Writing reflectively becomes an engaging experience that brings me calm, and amazingly, opens up a myriad of spiritual adventures.

Just imagine being able to access the benefits for yourself too. If you have forgotten yourself or can't find your true self, journaling can lead you to answers. My wish is to help you so that you can be on your way to gaining insights, accessing deeper truths and connecting with purpose.

Journaling puts you on an epic path of self-discovery.
You begin from where you are by starting with basic questions before diving in to find the parts of you that you had left behind, repressed or abandoned. A journaling review helps you to break down – shedding layers that do not serve you in your life and that does not reflect who you really are. Yet, it also involves a tremendous act of building up – recognizing who you can be.

Through journaling, if you find yourself identifying something that you'd like to change about yourself or your life, make a plan for it to happen. Real transformation only happens when you follow up with actions. By undertaking actions, you are on the way to creating a life that you'd love.

The key to solving the ache in your soul: *know yourself.*

"You have no need to travel anywhere. Journey within yourself, enter a mine of rubies and bathe in the splendor of your own light." Rumi

Knowing your core or authentic self helps you to navigate life in a way that supports your wellness. With better answers and self-knowledge, the path that you forge ahead becomes a lot clearer. You become way happier, not just temporarily but in a way that sustains.

Obviously, just completing the number of journal prompts in this guidebook alone is not going to offer you all the answers. Neither can they cover every aspect there is to know about your multi-dimensional sparkly personality. However, they are enough to set you off on a good start, in your self-discovery journey.

You are the carrier of truth when you allow God or Spirit to move through you. What you will be awakened by is the download of inspired ideas, visions, poems, and stories. *You will never be the same again when you journal from a place of authenticity, courage, and love.*

Awaken, Activate and Access Your Sacred Feminine Power

You are life seeking to renew itself. Your task is to awaken, activate and access your Sacred Feminine Power in its expression. Knowing yourself will ultimately lead you to purpose. You know who you are, why you are here and the difference that you can make in the world.

When you align with your Feminine Energy, you are not

just doing it for yourself. You are also doing it for future generations. It's a legacy that you create.

"Every woman who heals herself heals all the women who came before her, and all those who came after her." Chrstine Northrup

Through your womb, you hold the consciousness of creation. Your heart, the qualities for creativity, compassion, nurture, intuition, connection, patience, receptivity, and higher emotions. And your bosom, the capacity to nourish life.

Get in front of the mirror and love the person that you are. Bring out the fabulous from your divine feminine! Be awakened to your power with self-discovery.

Not just soul awakening, you want to activate and access your power so that you continuously shine! When you awaken, activate and access your Sacred Feminine Power, the following is what happens…

Awakening your Sacred Feminine Power empowers you to be able to stand in your own ground. You know that you can be who you are and that you do not need to hide behind any man's back. Neither do you need to play victim or engage in any manipulative games for getting ahead.

Activating your Sacred Feminine Power lets you tap into your creative abilities. You are able to design your life in the way you would like it to be. To manifest this life, you draw on your innate beautiful feminine nature: intuitive, graceful, nurturing, loving, knowing, compassionate, wise and sensuous. You are the dancer, the artist and the composer in a song of creation.

Accessing your Sacred Feminine Power means leading from the truth of your being, in alignment with your highest potential. For you carry the entire cosmos in your soul. You are the bringer of new beginnings and a force of change. Your purpose is to shine the light that you are, toward making a positive impact on the world. And you are Divine Love, through and from within.

From Sacred Self-Discovery to Tapping into Source

Ultimately, it is not just your human self that you'd come to know. Should you stay meditatively present to what's left, even after putting away the pen, you can possibly connect with a stream of consciousness.

It is a vast spiritual stream opens up. A field that that appears infinite. An experience that feels cosmic-like, even as you descend deeper within.

Interestingly, while you journey into this expanded space, you are called to let go of all your ego attachments, the 10,000 material things that you have identified yourself with, the name that you have always known yourself by and the female form that you are in.

In letting go, you become free. Free to explore without any pre-conceived ideas, labels or mistaken beliefs. Free to finally unravel the mystery of soul creation.

It is in this space of conscious awareness that the answer to the question that you seek lie: *who am I?*

As spiritual masters say, when you finally recall who you are on the inside, everything about you and your life changes.

Wishing you the very best in your journey inwards and with much love,

Evelyn Lim

Claim Your Free Gifts

To thank you for your purchase of my book, I'd like to offer you two complimentary gifts…

[Bonus #1] Downloadable List of 250 Journal Questions and Writing Prompts

Get the entire list of 250 Journal Questions laid out nicely in a document for your easier reference. Enjoy the convenience of making entries in a journal book of your choice or for creating an online journal.

[Bonus #2] Download 101 Positive Affirmations for Your Divine Feminine

Would like to support your Divine Feminine with positive affirmations? I'd like to offer you a list of 101 affirmations that you can use. Erase any old limiting beliefs and start saying positive words inwards. Nourish your mind with healthy thoughts that will bring out the best in your Divine Feminine!

How to Claim Your Free Gifts

To claim your gifts, fill out your name and email address when you click over the link below…

https://www.EvelynLim.com/claim-divine-feminine-gifts

Check Out Other Books

1. Abundance Alchemy Manifesto: A Guide to Finding Your Path, Manifesting with Purpose, and Living Life Fully

2. Self-Love Secrets: How to Love Yourself Unconditionally, Heal Your Heart Chakra and Feel Better Fast

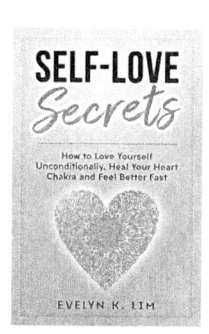

3. The Artists' Way by Julia Cameron

4. The Gifts of Imperfection: Let Go of Who You Think You're Supposed to Be and Embrace Who You Are by Brene Brown

About The Author

International coach, author, entrepreneur, energy healer and mother of two lovely girls, Evelyn Lim once faced inner struggle because she believed that she was "not good enough" after leaving her fast-paced banking career. She had found it difficult to love herself due to her negative self-talk and from not feeling worthy. Yet, she wanted to design a life whereby she can thrive from doing the work that she loves, make a difference in the world and still have time for her family. Well, she finally found her answers.

She has now dedicated her life to helping women feel empowered, so that they can shine their unique core brilliance. Her proven signature system takes those who are feeling stressed, release their past and to break free from their limiting beliefs. She specializes in helping women renew their energy levels, so that they can magnify their vision and ultimately align with their highest potential. Her proven system has created results; with her clients reporting greater wellness, improved relationships, and income breakthroughs; amongst others.

Evelyn is the author to the book "Abundance Alchemy Manifesto" and "Self-Love Secrets". She is also the co-author to "Adventures in Manifesting: Success and Spirituality" together with other well-known authors such as Dr. Joe Vitale and Dr. Fred Alan Wolf (teachers from The Secret), and Dr. Brian Tracy. She is also an avid reader of self-help books by other authors.

Evelyn intends to live her best life, and by doing so, inspire others to do the same. She'd be happy to share her ideas with you too. Learn to transform your results from the inside-out - while finding love in all that you are, do and have - and be empowered to support your family.

To read her articles and learn more about her, please click over to https://www.EvelynLim.com/blog.

Printed in Great Britain
by Amazon